ISBN: 978-1-942500-83-4

Boulevard Books
The New Face of Publishing

LASAGNA W/APPLESAUCE

Pete Kearney

Midas Aside

My years behind bars have made me a pro at sitting still. I can death stare your ass in any weight class. In a No Blink duel - I won't blink.

I spent sixty months in a cell with less ambience than this Midas waiting room. The boss has asked me to take the shop car in for brakes. I plop down on Old Sparky and pass my hand over weathered magazines. The TV is on but the sound off. There's a water cooler with paper cups and a unisex bathroom. Not enough room to swing a dead cat but compared to where I was this place is Caesars Palace.

The only thing I know about brakes is you have to have them. How long this job takes, I really don't care. I'm on the clock. I heard whispers about the boss trusting a car to a dude who did time- as if incarceration made me forget how to drive.

I set my boney elbows on my boney knees and stare past my interlaced fingers. They morph into Greco-Roman wrestlers as I focus behind them to lock on a spot on the floor. The deaf-mute weather girl is ignored. No distraction will pollute the sincerity of my waiting. Nobody gets paid to watch TV. I'm engaged in professional sitting still, a job I was trained to do.

I read somewhere that everybody should try to convince themselves that the present moment is the best time of their life. If you're on a downhill descent and your brakes fail it's going to be a challenge.

My X-ray vision is melting a square of waiting room carpet. I sit so still I go out of body. Taking a think break, I study the air in front of my eyes as light seeps into my frame. Hours and minutes are alike. People come to pick up or drop off their cars. No one dares my waiting room.

As guest of the state I had the kind of time to memorize Shakespeare. I can do the Saint Crispin's Day speech as a morning prayer and Marc Anthony as a nightcap. Unlocking my eyes helps me memorize.

The Service Manager Doug, assures me my car is up next. His arm ink looks like it was done in the can.

"No hurry." I say. Doug has a mullet.

"Where did you learn to sit so still? Doug asks.

"Auburn." I guess he's done time.

"I was at Downstate." We went to different prisons together.

"Your Boss told you this car had no brakes?"

"Not really. I found out on the drive here."

"You had to come down Hillside?"

"I would have wrecked with anyone in front of me."

"Why would your boss ask you to do that?"

"Good question."

Embezzlement is not a word you want on your resume. Because I skimmed the state I repaid the state. I didn't steal anything from you or anyone you know. My boss did me a "big" favor putting me on his crew. I'm in a haz-mat suit killing bed bugs. Try to find people who want this kind of work. Then he asks me to take a car with no brakes downtown. He must really like me.

7

Driving back with brand new shoes, every brake tap swirls the dashboard Hula Girl. I whiplash at red lights. I won't dare drive-thru food. Midas has super-sized these brakes. The pedal is so high my knee hits the steering column. I stop so quick I'm nearly rear-ended. I've flipped the sand clock from no stop to stop short.

I suspect the boss sees me in a new light since our audit. As the lone convicted felon on his staff I'm an in-house fall guy. If I were to go away on short notice recent imbalances might be easier to explain.

I knock at the boss's door.

"Car's back, the brakes are way high.

"Didn't Doug warn you?"

"I found out on the way back.

"I have something I need you to do."

"People are going to talk."

"Tomorrow 0800 bring your haz-mat gear."

When you debug bed bugs in the home of a wealthy rapper there are drugs and cash to consider. The client insists on holding a gun on me while I work. Everybody at the shop assumes I'm the guy for this call. I've never had a gun pointed at me until I got into extermination. I'm a white-collar criminal.

Two days after I sprayed the cluttered duplex the boss calls me in his office.

"There's a ring missing from Apac's apartment."

"Bullshit – he was watching me every minute"

"He said you took off your mask to swallow something."

"His ring?' I take a chair.

"Her ring."

"His wife leaves a diamond ring laying around?"

"Did I say 'diamond?'"

"He's sure it's you. He's on his way with detectives."

"Are they going to strain my stool?"

"He's suing our parent company so he's going to need you to confess. The insurance company pays because we sent a convicted felon into the man's home.

"What's my share?"

"No one presses charges. The ring is never recovered."

"The ring doesn't exist."

"I like the way you catch on."

"I assume I'm fired. I'll need severance."

"He has an envelope."

"For me or us."

"For us. Don't worry – it's in an account.

"You know I'm on parole."

"For now, you are."

Galley Tales

The black mess cook Robinson claims he once went twenty-one days without a bowel movement. The topic has been Filipina women so his change of subject provokes the assembled waitstaff.

"You're more full of crap now, than you were then."

Nestle bar dark in spotless kitchen whites, Robinson slips off a server table and takes the floor. He rebukes his sink crew as if addressing a Roman forum.

"You, cracker mother-fathers expect me to listen to your bullshit but when I state a fact you go Perry Mason. Can't a black man tell a story?"

I feel for him. Robinson doesn't often get involved in bull sessions. Now he does and nobody gives a shit about his can't take a shit story. I scold my mates.

"Guys, let the dude tell his story. We've got time to kill before chow. Robby, can you do something with the twenty-one days? Can it be fifteen? That bullshit we might believe."

"Twenty-one days!" Robinson steps toward me and I step back. We are friends, mess cooking buddies, pool table teammates. Not every black guy will buddy up with a white guy.

Robinson puts on his pastor voice.

"I sweated every one of those twenty-one nights. I dreamt of cake decorating, snakes molting and a submarine launch."

"Your wet dream was dropping anchor." I chime in.

"I don't need your help." Robinson rolls his eyes up like Lotto balls.

"Sorry."

"Believe it or not Mates, I prayed. I got on my knees and begged for relief. My gut was a sack of spackle. I felt ready to go but I couldn't pull the trigger."

"You never heard of laxatives?"

"I found out a gypsy had cast a spell on me because she thought I cheated on her daughter."

"We're gonna need waders if this shit gets any deeper." One voice speaks for us all.

"Go ahead mates, make fun. I promise you, go through something like I did and you will know there is dark magic hidden in every corner of the world.

'How did you know a spell was cast on you?"

"A psychic saw the curse in a teacup?"

"Was she Filipina?" I'm trying to get back to where we were before Robbie made his constipation claim.

"My tour is almost up. Can we get to the punchline?" A voice echoes off the deep sink

"On the twenty first night of the curse I was driven mad. I had tried every remedy, homemade and over the counter. I turned to a vet who worked at a cattle ranch."

"He stuck his hand up your ass?" Robinson ignores the catcall.

"Guys who mucked stalls for a living turned their pitchforks in when they saw the movement I dropped on the deck of that horse barn. I walked home on tip toe. Suddenly I could dunk a basketball."

"So, what got you unplugged?"

"Horse piss, hot as soup in a cup. I knocked back enough to have it shoot through my system pushing out everything in front of it."

"Great, horse piss, no one is gonna top that before chow." I raise Robbie's hand in a majority decision over whatever else we might have talked about.

Faces are appearing at the window of the galley. Early birds often eat twice.

The Play That Never Works

ACT ONE

The snow slows to a stop. A busboy comes outside
and pokes the restaurant awning with a
broomstick. It recreates the storm in fast forward.
On his way inside he flips the door sign to OPEN.

Two winos clear enough snow in front of the OTB to
lay down a cardboard magic carpet. They sit close
to share a bottle. Backs against the window they
recline as snow drifts.

Big Mac and Joe Camel sit in an idling unmarked.
The snow-covered car suggests a stakeout from an
igloo with its windshield wipers on. They are
waiting for Izzy Matos, a repeat offender who bets
the horses. They suspect him too superstitious to
change his window.

Izzy arrives in a thrift store mink and a blonde wig.

    "We should let him walk around like that."
Joe notes Izzy's head is on a swivel.

When Izzy hears Mac open the car door he bolts
toward the subway steps. Unsteady on lady boots
he slips in the snow and gets cuffed. Onlookers look

on from inside the front window of Tad's Steakhouse. Mac and Joe put him in their car. A domestic abuser is off the street.

The things we can't make fun of have power over us. Joe Camel knows this true. The instincts that make him an effective cop make him a good human being. He accepts his tag because he knows he has no choice. You don't get to pick your nickname.

Prior to the Academy, Joe boxed in the basement of the Lost Battalion Hall on Queens Boulevard. He was one on a dance floor of jabbing welterweights. At an amateur event he wanted to be announced as Least of the Lost. His coach said no. He fought as Joe Leastski, a name that now exists only on his birth certificate.

Joe Camel's partner Big Mac is a six five, two hundred fifty-pound ready-made nickname. He enjoys a menu of advantages. Mac can go all day without seeing someone bigger than himself. His size has shaped his gentle temperament. He explained to the squad room that he'd never been in a street fight.

Paul McCracken was the junior varsity starting center his first year in high school. He snapped his way to a college scholarship and played in the Hula Bowl. Other than on every offensive play he rarely touched the ball.

In addition to a size advantage Paul was blessed by a seamless ascending trajectory of accomplishments that include a hamburger nickname. The big potholes in his life he dug for himself. He married outside his culture and wanted to write a play.

Mac's Mumbai wedding was a three-day success and a week of jet lag. There were no wedding costumes in Mac's size. He wore what they had and looked comical.   His sole preoccupation focused on a project that would derive no benefit from his body size. He wanted to write a three-act drama that played Broadway. The idea was stubborn as a blocking sled.

When he shared his frustration with his partners at the stationhouse they took turns teasing.

"Here he comes - Arthur Miller Lite."

ACT TWO

As a first-year uniform, Joe came upon a Christmas shopper being pistol-whipped. He chased the perp down two L shaped alleyways, the lights from the loading docks catching his rookie shoeshine. Emerging at Broadway and Dey he drew his service weapon and shot a bus shelter. The ad on the side was a camel extending a pack of filter-tips. Backlit by streetlight it appeared to Joe to be a man pointing a weapon.

"Enjoy your time off." His Captain sent him home for two weeks without pay. When he returned he was transferred to the 106th in southern Queens. His nickname arrived before him.

After a turn at the front desk Joe was matched with Mac and they shared a squad car. After night shifts they started playing handball at a park on 150th street. With the sun just up, they had the court to themselves. Big Mac could not accept being beat by a guy Joe's size.

"Don't take it too hard Mac. I've whipped guys bigger than you."

"You don't know anyone bigger than me."

"You want me to go easy on you Andre?"

"You could talk less."

Mac started playing a "rainbow" style of handball that featured arcing shots that allowed him time to interfere with Joe's returns. It made the games competitive.

Resting between games the two were approached by a teen with new Nikes.

"Got kicks for sale."

In the park parking lot, they joined a group of people huddled around the open side of a panel van. Inside two teens scrambled over the cartons pulling out boxes of sneakers while shoppers called out color and size. An older man collected money and urged everyone to be quick. Two others were obvious lookouts. Orange Danza lot labels were sunlit by the open door. Only Joe bought. When they returned they had to play local kids who had taken over the court while they were away.

Monday, Joe spoke to the import manager at Danza who was unaware he was short one hundred cartons of sneakers from a Taiwan consolidation. Joe ran the van plate and a patrol car started off to an address in Ozone Park. Seventy cartons, cross-tiered on a pallet, were found in the garage and three people were arrested.

The 106th Captain shaking hands with the president of the JFK Brokers Association was the next front cover of the Airport Press. The mayor called to congratulate all involved. Big Mac made detective. He and Joe got assigned as plainclothes handball players.

Over the summer, the two undercovers made deals with cargo thieves working the JFK backstretch. They carried cash and haggled as if it were their own. Joe suggested to the locals that he and Mac were friends of an organization in Howard Beach. It was easy to see a guy Mac's size as a mob bodyguard and Joe as a low-level wise guy. The intensity they devoted to handball made their cover convincing.

ACT THREE

Paul McCracken won a college writing contest for a two-act play, <u>In the Unlikely Event of a Water Landing</u>. No one could recall a two-act play written by a football player. It gave Mac the idea that the novelty could make him the next Broadway Joe. On or off Broadway he imagined hearing his words made flesh; bitter truths whispered from the lips of beautiful women and ironic asides from their foils.

The ambition followed Mac through the Academy into plainclothes. People remarked on his luck. Mac tempered everything in the light of wanting to write a three-act play. It kept him humble - a quality that made him the good cop in the good cop bad cop equation.

Izzy slouches in the posture of a man handcuffed from behind.

"Why did you beat up your old lady?' Joe asks.

"She wasn't listening."

"That again."

Mac pulls a script from beneath his seat.

"Izzy, I have a story about a guy who hits on a bet so big he's afraid to claim it. I need OTB details."

"Any story involving betting horses I can make authentic. What do I get for my advice?"

"We're gonna say you turned yourself in." Joe is as anxious as Mac to get this play writing started.

"Give me a seat at the stationhouse and I'll make notes. If this guy is a regular player he would have made multiple bets."

"Say, he's overheard something. He has an idea that people know he's hit big." Joe can tell Mac is making this up while driving.

"You guys came out in the snow to get me?"

"We heard you helped the Puerto Rican kid with his Broadway musical."

"He's from Barbados. He took my advice on a few things."

"Talk to me, Izzy. I need an angle about a longshot this guy fears claiming. Write in English. Don't be creative. Tell me why you thought your bet today was worth dressing in drag to make."

"I was avoiding arrest or hoped I was." Izzy wiggles over his cuffs. "Am I getting paid?"

The 106th sits in a toe of Queens that pools after a routine rain. Mac ferries his dispatcher across the flooded parking lot. She's twenty- three and slender enough to carry like a bride. Cops watching, curse his good fortune.

"I hope his play never works."

Handball rules reside with courtside old-timers. Some claim you must stay at the long line until the serve hits the wall. Others allow you to move up shoulder to shoulder with the server. No rule prohibits you from standing at the short line two steps forward of the server. Mac insists that anything not prohibited is allowed. His shadow throws a shape on the wall that mimics target man at the firing range. Bouncing side to side he recreates the shadows of old Yankee Stadium. Joe fires his serves at Mac's face and more often than not they are swatted down with Kong-like high-fives. Mac starts winning more than ever before. Springing from his center position, Mac kills low serves.

"I've found a play that works." Mac takes a bow.

Joe applauds. "We're in Jackson Heights but it is Broadway."

Frogman in a Tree

It's pouring rain and the sun is shining. We are moving uphill through waist-high dry grass crisscrossed with mud paths slippery as baby shit. I'm one in a conga line of men searching for sniper nests in the Central Highlands. We are blowing up holes in the ground on my hundredth day at the show.

Despite the poncho, I'm soaked to the dog tags. One thought crowds out all others; me separating from my group and taking my boot off. The space between the two small toes on my left foot is oozing infection. Every step is a handshake with a clown. Shooting pain is constant as a car alarm. If I don't take this boot off my head is going to explode.

Jungle rot, flesh eating bacteria, angry microbes attack me at my most remote location. My two smallest digits are besieged as much as that fated French fort.

If you take your boot off while in the bush you're subject to court martial. Everyone knows your foot will swell and you won't be able to get the boot back on. You're not going to hump on one foot. You can't be left behind so the whole unit will have to await a dust off. I can't take my boot off- I would never hear the end of it.

The sniper holes are so small they're not worth destroying. Captain Trell opts to leave a one-man recon. "Frogman, in a tree," he's looking at me. I have my mouth open.

"Kane starts R&R tomorrow. You get the sleepover. Don't start any shit, we won't be back till daylight."

Kane is our outfit hard ass. I'm flattered the Captain chose me to replace him. If Kane can sleep in a tree so can I. From my perch I watch my unit descend the hill. Sunlight flashes off unsecured gear. I could pick off two of my own guys if I was a sniper for the other side.

They call me Frogman because I flopped out of the Navy Seals. On a distance swim off Puerto Rico I was stung by a man-o-war. By the time I recovered, I was expected to re-up or return to the fleet. An intra-service transfer got me into the infantry. The Army was looking for a few million men.

I drop down from where I was boosted up and scramble into the bush. Determined as a game show contestant, I unlace while my head swivels. Tugging on the boot. I break wind loud enough to give away my location. The foot swells while I watch. My sock peels off like sunburn. I hold it up as a steaming tea bag. My foot is white as a bar of bath soap. The two infected digits are raisin brown and entwined like drowning swimmers.

"I may have to leave you two in country." I console my toes. "Casualties of a ground war."

Rubbing my thumb between my toes, I wipe a black snot on my pantleg. My ears pop. I know it won't last long but it will last a little while. My foot looks like a loaf of French bread. No way can I put my boot back on.

An ashtray of crushed butts banging together like bumper cars is how I imagine my foot rot under a microscope. The split between my toes is deep enough to stitch. This is no ordinary jungle rot oozing up. I consider it an open wound. If I didn't act my head might have exploded. I have a taste of metal in my mouth.

On the ground with my back against a tree, my foot is cradled atop its empty boot. I'm giving the dog the night off. All I have to do is breathe until daylight and if I sleep – sleep with one eye open.

I'm no sick call sissy. I can endure pain as well as the next guy. Some of my crew bitch about bug bites. Bubin claims his balls itch so bad it makes his eyes water. I bet him he couldn't stand a watch without digging his hands in his pants - easiest money I ever made.

I met my squad at Benning. Half the guys fed the camp mice while the others went to war against them. The first night there I lay awake listening to traps snap in the dark barracks. In the morning I was assigned to do a body count. I was the new guy.

"Anything we kill is the enemy" I was advised.

Now that I'm not the new guy I like everyone but the new new guy. Sitting alone in the bush, I'm an occupying force, a boot on the ground.

Someone running downhill and breathing heavy passes by me, looks back and slips on their ass. Grabbing my loose boot, I slide down and capture her. I hold the open boot to the side of her head while I cover her mouth with my other hand. Her attempt to escape improves my hold on her. I take her back to the tree where I left my weapon.

"No V.C." She is young and pretty. Someone has to be looking for her.

I assume she is with whoever is digging those holes. I place her in front of me in a bobsled formation. My bare foot atop my empty boot and we relax backward. It is starting to rain.

She must be up here supplying info or entertaining a VC cadre. There is no way I can let her go. She's my prisoner- the first I've ever had.

Rain on my swollen foot is a relief. I pull her closer to me and I can feel her heart racing. With no sound of persuers I relax my grip. She seems less afraid of me than whoever is chasing her.

From a small sack at her hip she draws out a bottle with an eyedropper top. Without asking she applies drops to my blackened toes and passes a ice cream stick coated with charcoal between them.

"God has sent me a VC visiting nurse." I offer a prayer of Thanksgiving. Pain lifts as a mist.

The rain lets up, I turn my poncho inside out and we lie beside each other close as toes. My hand slips under her arm and cups a breast beating like a bird There is no way I can be found with my boot off and a woman beside me. I'll let her go at daylight and hope my outfit doesn't find her.

Over the course of the night we come to a peace agreement. Kissing leads to careful moving around. For one night in a long war, I get to love my enemy.

Captain Trell finds me out of my lookout nook

"Came down to crap."

"You're in a good mood."

"101 days at the show."

"You're not short if you can't count down."

I have the back of my boot sliced open and my foot jammed inside. Every step is a step on a Lego.

Bubin waits until the Captain walks away. He shows me my sock on the tip of his knife.

"You want me to stay quiet about this?"

"Forget about what you owe me."

"Anything you want to tell me Frogman?"

"Nothing that you would believe."

Front Desk

Every overnight doorman draws the Old Maid card once in his career. An episode arising in the unforgiving small hours when time is measured with the second hand. Perhaps a resident returning from a debauchery pukes in the lobby or a pissed off door-dash keys the elevator. As doorman you owe it to the board to observe, report and when possible react. You have no authority except the authority you assign yourself. It's not your place to tell people who live in the building how to behave. You work for them. You're a security guard, concierge and a door opener. Be aware of your place on the food chain. You got the job because you wear a white shirt and a tie.

I quit a building of 83 apartments and 210 residents all of whom I pretty much got along with. I had the good sense to remark if a woman just had her hair done. I've listened to stories that involved no one I knew and nothing I cared about. If trapped in a long recounting, I can use my phone to make the desk phone ring. Tenants come to me with complaints I can't do anything about other than acknowledge them. I can offer a weather report, a take-out menu or a postage stamp.

I'm not one of those union doormen dressed as Captain Kangaroo who actually opens the door. I sit at a desk and at an appropriate hour I put my feet up on it. When the phone rings I answer "Front desk". If I don't get up and fluff the pillows on the lobby couch, sleep can creep up on me. I'm babysitting a building of dreamers headed toward another day of working at a real job.

Everything came to a head after a beautiful Hindu woman took an apartment with her aging mother. I make the prayer hands greeting when I see them and drop an "Acha" into an exchange of pleasantries. A doorman should be aware of the cultures under his roof.

Two-ton Tony in 333 has a habit of hiring girls to visit. On occasion he comes down to meet the girl and escort her up. Other times he asks me to send her up. They always leave alone or sit in the lobby awaiting Uber.

The Hindu girl whose name is Anu rings me at 2AM to say she's called an ambulance. Her Mother is short of breath and complaining of chest pain.

As I escort the gurney through the lobby, one of the two EMTs does a double-take over Tony's date of the night sitting on the couch reapplying make-up.

"You stinking slut." He slaps a compact mirror out her hand. I'm guessing he knows her but doesn't know everything about her. Without getting up the girl stabs him in the groin with a UFC leg kick spearheaded by a spiked heel. The EMT goes to his knees then folds until his head touchs the floor. His partner turns to me to do whatever comes next. The phone at the desk rings. I'm sure it's Anu.

"You better go up alone." I tell the EMT. "Her Mother is fading."

The escort stands over the fallen EMT.

"Stay out of this." She barks at me.

"You better go. Cops are going to be here

"Did you call them?"

"They follow the ambulances.".

The man on the floor moans.

"Is he your boyfriend?"

"Ex – thinks he can tell me what to do."

The elevator door opens, out comes Anu.

"I can't lift her alone!"

The EMT looks at his fallen comrade who has
rolled over onto his back without taking his hands
off his groin. Anu turns to me.

"What is this a party? My Mother is dying."
She looks at the distressed escort and then back to
me.

"Do something please."

"That's my car." The escort heads to the door
with her dress hiked up for running. On the way
out, she blows me a kiss.

"So long Sweetie."

Anu slumps in a chair and cries into her hands. I
get the EMT on his feet. Uniforms arrive and there

are plenty of hands to assist. If you need a party call 911.

Anu has a new look on her face. I can tell she thinks me incapable of being any help to her in the future. A beautiful woman knows you seek her approval and beautifully holds it back. Thank God her Mother didn't die. On that same night there was a false fire alarm and the newspaper guy got into a shoving argument with a limo driver that I had to referee. When the sun came up people ran from the building to catch the train. I drove home resolved to finding a new place to open doors.

Minolta 457

Mike Farley's first cold call follows nine weeks of sales training. At company headquarters he has rehearsed with classmates and instructors. As an outside Sales Associate he pursues a career in selling office copiers.

He targets Butts Realty, a fourth- floor real estate office in yellow office building. With his business card cocked he knocks on the door.

"Come in." It's a young woman.

"I'm here about your copier."

"Thank God, it's breaking down every other day. I have to beg to get a service call."

"I'm not repairing I'm selling. I can replace your unit with a Minolta 457 that comes with a special discount for any company in this building."

A young man with his tie untied enters from an inner office.

"What kind of discount?"

Mike hands the man his card and gets none in return. Sales reps are trained to keep the client's card in sight to insure they don't scramble a name. Not every Michael wants to be called Mike.

"I'm offering 15% off if I can get two sales in the same building."

"You'll have to talk to the boss and he's not here."

"Do you expect him back?"

"That prick walks out of the office without telling anyone where's he's going or when he'll be back."

In response to a horn blowing the man walks to the window.

"Are you driving a red car?"

"Yes." Mike joins the man at the window.

"You parked in the boss's spot."

"Oh sorry – it wasn't marked. I'll move it."

"You leave this office Mike and you've blown your sale. We're just about to order a copier."

"You are?"

"Get me a contract. The boss will have to park with the peons. Serves the bastard right."

"I don't mind moving my car."

"If you walk out of here - don't come back. I want you to sit with Susie and explain the features of your copier. She's the one who will be breaking it."

Mike sits at a breakroom table with Susie. Their knees touch. Her perfume makes him sneeze.

"God bless you." Her smile is sweet and her eyelashes artificial.

The office door flies open and papers lift off the reception desk.

"God dammit; Susie call those elevator people. I'm not climbing those stairs again." The boss is out of breath and crossing the office like a finish line.

"This young man is selling us a new copier." Susie stands to explain.

"Did you park in my spot?" Mike stands to answer.

"Sorry Sir. I'll run down and move it."

"You can't I've blocked you in."

"I apologize but the spot wasn't marked."

"Listen to me son. I don't know how long you've been in the working world but the parking spot closest to the entrance is not for a copier salesman."

"Again, I'm sorry. Let me have your keys and I'll move your car.

"No freaking way are you touching my car. Who the hell are you."

'Mike Farley, Minolta Copiers." Mike extends his card.

The boss takes the card as if to verify the name.

"Well I'm not leaving till 4pm so you can sit here till then."

"Sir, I have other appointments."

"Do you? Tough break but if I'm buying a copier I need more info. You need to go over everything with Susie after lunch."

"I have to complete four calls a day."

"Bullshit!" The boss picks up a phone but doesn't dial. "Can I speak to the manager?" He pauses to read Mike's card.

"My name is Elmer Butts I run Butts Realty, your rep Mike Farley is here in my office. First of all, he's parked in my spot, now he refuses to explain the features of the unit to our receptionist. I need a copier but no way in hell will I ever buy a Minolta. Fire this motherfather or I'll sue you for sending him over here."

"Now Mike, you don't want me making that call do you? Just sit with Susie. Don't try to fuck her or us. We want a good unit with lots of operator instruction. Susie has burned through three copiers her first year here."

Pizza comes. Mike and Susie sit in the breakroom. Everyone else eats at their desks.

"Are you single, asking for a friend" Susie's smile is straight, her hair frames a face pretty as a cat.

"Engaged sorta." Mike stutters.

"Do you want to go out with me.'

"Sure, what would like to do.

"Fuck, after whatever we do first."

"You are a very forward."

"See how you catch on?"

"What about the copier."

"I don't have a copier temperament. I'll need you to make service visits. Some days I'm alone here with nothing to do."

"We're not going to talk about collating after this conversation."

"Mr. Butts left. Your car is free." The man with his tie undone sticks his head in the office.

"Did he say he was coming back."

"Again - with this?

A horn is blaring. Mike Farley runs down four floors – elevator still out. He trips at a landing and scrapes a hole in the knee of his best suit. He's left the contract upstairs with his old school schoolbag. Outside, the car with the horn is not the boss. Once he backs out, the car with the horn takes the boss's spot. Driving off the property in search of a parking spot it occurs to him to just go home.

Persistence overcomes resistance is the first and last thing they sell in sales school. Mike starts the walk back to the office. The only spot he can find is a block and a half away.

A car pulls alongside him and the window comes down.

"What are you doing?" It's Elmer Butts.

"I took my car out of your spot."

"Idiot, I told my son-in-law to have you wait until I got back. Now some other asshole will park there."

"Can I ride with you."

"Fuck no." Mike sees his reflection in the rising passenger window.

He climbs the stairs out of breath. His schoolbag is outside the office door. The son-in-law with the untied tie answers Mike's knock. He explains that the boss is on a conference call and Susie is busy with a copier repairman.

"If you want to wait, please wait downstairs."

Jerry's Gold

I wake up thinking about precious metals. Maybe today is a day to buy silver. I don't know where to go to buy it or how to buy it and the money I have I'm saving for breakfast. Gold too, I ought to get gold.

My Godfather put the thought in my head. It took a few weeks to filter past more immediate concerns and in the wake of my waking up I replay his advice.

We're at the annual family picnic with beer and barbeque. Jerry pulls me aside and suggests I devote a piece of each paycheck to a gold certificate

"Do I look like I need money? Don't answer."

I'm drinking one beer while holding another beer to the side of my head where my brother-in-law spiked a volleyball. "By accident."

"You start small when you're young."

"I get the joke Jer – I know you don't feel well. I mean you mean well."

I'm deaf in the ear where I was hit by the ball. I hear a horseshoe clang and screams from the egg toss but anything closer is mute. Drinking after being struck in the head is making me feel unsafe to drive. Why am I drinking a warm beer while holding a cold beer to my head? I've picked up an abandoned Bud.

Jerry's the family comedian, why the financial advice? What this year we get no jokes? Voices of my family rise and fall, for a few seconds I'm lip-reading Jerry.

"Someone said the only thing to do with advice is give it." I'm moving off subject.

Jerry is not the kind of Godfather who puts a dollar in your pocket when you're growing up. Now he's giving me a commercial from late night radio.

"Jerry- you heard about the fur sale?"

"You're telling me jokes I told you."

"A dyslexic walks into a bra..." I'm trying to jumpstart Jerry.

"It's great that you're a wiseass but think about providing for your family."

"You think I'm broke because I have two jobs?"

'Invest some energy in a long-term plan."

"I have to find a something colder to drink. Can I get you anything?"

"Don't run away. This is life. We will not be having this talk at next year's picnic."

"Promise."

"You have no idea about Quantitative Easing?"

"What did you call me?"

"Situations arise when you're not prepared for them." Jerry squeezes my arm.

"Jerry -we're at a party. Where's the jokes."

"I have cancer."

'Oh crap. Are you serious?"."

"I know I never put any money in your pocket when you were a kid. Hey I had my own kids to worry about. While I'm still here I'd like know you're headed in the right direction. Take my advice you won't be sorry."

"Who have you told?"

"About gold?'

"About your cancer."

'Only you."

"Thanks -why?"

"Open out of town.

"Are you going to die."

"I might make Christmas."

"Jerry, thanks for your concern about my future. Why hit me with this cancer thing? My eardrum is humming from that volley ball. Where is that kid, I should spike his drink."

"Was he the Korean volleyball player, Spike Lee?"

"Good Jerry – you're getting warm."

"I can't ask anyone else to crack jokes at my wake."

"Is that what I'm doing?"

"I have prepared material for you to use when the time comes."

"Sure, I'll dress it up."

"Please don't."

"Well I'm flattered to be asked and I promise to start my own gold portfolio as a tribute to your great confidence in me."

"So, we've made some progress." Jerry walks away and starts telling my cousins a joke about a duck.

Anonymous

A guy named Anonymous wrote a lot of dirty books; paperbacks built to fit a sailor's dungarees, the salesman's coat pocket and perhaps a lady's pocketbook. Not the erotic literature of Fanny Hill or The Pearl but popcorn porn popped from an Olivetti Aristocrat.

Anonymous created a cheat sheet of scenes and phrases intended to aid in masturbation. Plot outcomes are prescribed as lion eats wildebeest. The reader reads quick, anxious to get to what he knows is coming.

When Anonymous first opened shop he recruited talent from a community college creative writing class. They would get paid by the page for cranking out basic ring the doorbell and screw stories. He would outline the plot and pay them to fill it in with scenes designed to titillate his audience of wankers, stroke bookies and one-handed readers.

Ralph is assigned to write a story about a hot librarian who walks in on her boss getting oral from a girl in return for his forgiving her late fees.

Ralph's considers himself an artist. He goes on and on about the librarian's ears. The first three pages are her rubbing oil on her lobes and easing studs in and out.

"Someone should get laid within the first ten pages." The boss walks the sidelines as a porn coach.

"I'm having that sewn on a pillow." Ralph never takes his eyes off his typewriter. At fifty cents a page he can't waste whiteout.

The boss raps his knuckles on the writer's table.

"Okay team at ease, I want to emphasize spelling and grammar but I'm not going to waste your time. I'm seeing a bit of creativity slip into our product. There's no need to set a story in outer space. Keep it simple sex. Sew that on a pillow."

When Anonymous reviews the first fifty pages of Ralph's script he is dismayed to find the blowjob isn't even over. He takes Ralph aside.

"I would hate to lose you."

"Trust me, you'll get over it."

"Can't you save this shit for your writing class."

"I've dropped out."

"Why.'

"I wasn't getting paid."

"Well I am paying you and I want you to write the way I've asked you to. You're not going to make a name for yourself on my back. Everything is published by Anonymous. Your twisting your whistle if you think anyone will know this is your work."

"I understand." Ralph is in love with his librarian character and determined to save her from a book club gang bang.

"I'll pay you for these pages even though they are not what I wanted. Get back to the girl on her knees, Ralph. What kind of books did she find so hard to return? How high were those fees? Was the boss aware she had Anais Nin out for three months? This little tramp is begging to get her hair pulled. Take it from there Ralph but for God's sake get somebody laid."

"Aye Aye Captain." Ralph resolves to turn his heroine into a whore in tribute to the part librarians   have played in stimulating literature.

Soupy Shoe Sales

Sal's Shoe Shine boasts three high chairs, two
celebrity photos and an ad for Cat's Paw. Were
Soupy Sales and George Gobel regulars here? I
never got the truth. Sal said the pictures were
there when he bought the place. The cobbler that
came with the shop didn't speak English. People
have asked me about them and then bit their
tongues because I'm blind. Soupy could be sitting
next to you and I couldn't confirm it.

People get a kick from getting their shoes shined by
a blind man. When the NY Post did a story on me,
Sal taped it on our front window. I became a
neighborhood celebrity. Kids were calling me Shoe
Magoo. After channel Four did a feature on me I
spent a month ducking Ernie Arnastos. I'm legally
blind but I'm not totally blind so I keep what I see
to myself. Eventually I'll be just as blind as the
next blind guy.

When I first put my nose up close to those photos I
saw Soupy and George both wore bowties. It
inspired me.   Ask me where you can get your shoes

shined in Staten Island by a blind man wearing a bowtie?

The other shines take the rush hour shifts. I work in the dead of the afternoon. My regulars include a Filipino pastor who thinks because I'm blind I can't hear. He wears cowboy boots for which we should charge extra but he's a good tipper so Sal lets him slide.

Blind people rely on others to count their money. At the end of a shift I have the Hindu who does heels and soles sort my tips- twenties in a back pocket, singles in my shirt. Fives and tens, I turn into twenties. I'm at the mercy of others until they make cash braille.

It's thirty-three steps from my door to the curb. Hang a right, tap my stick for forty steps and I'm at the bus that drops me across the street from Sal's. There's an audible crosswalk but folks insist on helping me. I don't stand in the way of people doing good.

My brushes and rags are arranged precise as a surgery theatre. I shine while the Pastor yells at his phone.

"Gomez, you don't know how to return a call? I'm at Sal's, getting a shine. Call me. You better have the girl with you."

Over months of eavesdropping I've figured out the Pastor has a business of sponsoring Filipina girls to work as au pairs. It's none of my business if the work they wind up doing is one-hour massage. I've heard him say it takes a year to cover the cost of importing a girl.

Sal bought his shoe shop with money won at the track. Now he can disguise losses on his income tax return. He doesn't ask me how much I make. Until the story in the Post he was thinking of charging me to work here. I was a postman until my eyes turned against me. People on my route would remark on my well-shined shoes.

Estrella comes into the shop announced by her perfume. She asks me if I know where the Pastor is."

"Not today, have you tried his church?"

"His church is in Manila," the sweet voice of a Filipina speaking English.

"I didn't know that. He's a regular here but he hasn't been in this week."

"He was supposed to pick me up at the airport. I had to take a cab to his place and his landlady said he's in some kind of trouble with the police. She thought he might be here." She's standing near enough that I can smell her hair spray.

"You have no place to stay."

"It seems that way." She's small enough that her words address my shirt pocket.

"Take a seat dear, you must be exhausted."

"I have a cab outside."

"Have him put your bags in the foyer." I count out five back pockets.

It crosses my mind she might take my money and leave in the cab. She comes back in and hands me change.

She gets up in my chair and I take off her shoes. Her stockings are damp with a smell of world travel. I brush up her loafers and sprinkle talc inside them.

"I'm going to take care of you until we find the Pastor."

"Why would you do that?"

"Don't stand in the way of a person doing a good deed."

"He's arranged a job for me with a local family. I'm

supposed to start the first of the month."

"Welcome to America." I lock up my toolbox. I'm taking her home.

She takes my arm at the crosswalk. The bus drivers on my route all know me. When we board the driver whistles.

"Magoo, you got a keeper there."

"How would I know?"

At my place she gets in my bed. She's spent thirty-three hours in a coach seat.

"No need to worry my dear, I can't see a thing. She's refuses my offer of a hot shower.

By the time I've made tea she's snoring. I sit across the room listening to her sleep. She's a dark form suggesting a body bag. Her name is Estrella. I say it under my breath until it sounds like Australia.

I hear her on the phone with the Pastor. Refreshed by ten hours of sleep, she hands me the phone.

"Keep her with you. I'll cover your expenses. I'm being held on a warrant in Jersey. Don't tell anyone she's with you." This is the longest conversation I've had with this steady customer.

"One more thing Magoo. Don't try to fuck her."

"Never crossed my mind Pastor."

"Bullshit, you're blind not stupid."

That afternoon at the shop she watches me shine.
Men usually in a hurry are hanging around.
Estrella sits in a high chair, singing pop songs in
English. Men hand her money that might have
been my tip.

Estrella begins brushing at the chair on my right.
I'm not seeing the new customers but I'm hearing
them come in. I instruct her in wax and rag. The
Hindu complains that Estrella's low-cut blouses are
doubling customers but his salary is stalled. The
quality of her shine is never questioned. I press my
nose toward her chest to get an idea of what the
fuss is all about. Never have felt so sorry for myself.
Guys mute the Mets to talk to her.

"You're bigger than sports on T.V." I tease
her."

"Perhaps I'm not as attractive as you
imagine."

"You'll never get old around me."

Interview with a Redhead

Every Romeo wants a redhead on his resume.
Should she possess green eyes, ivory skin, and a
green sweater points will double. An 8 with red
hair is a10.

Every redhead has heard of Brenda Starr. The
hard-driving girl reporter in fashionable shoes. The
comics made a point of saying she was a redhead in
case the funnies bled before they reached you. The
censors cut a panel where Brenda smoked a polka
dot cigar. Her cleavage was erased. She was a 40's
girl pursued by a freak with an eye patch -Basil St.
John.

Imagine spending your life having people comment
on your hair. Compliments impose on you, you're
expected to smile. It was not your idea. You didn't
ask for red hair. It's a blessing curse.

I saw a girl at the library. Her hair flowed behind
her in a lion's mane, red as red China. I pulled my
mask off and gawked. She passed me half a smile. I
guess she thought I was over doing it. Redheads
walk a red line between snobbism and stardom.

"What type of wine do people compare with the color of your hair?"

Dianne in a green V-neck leans forward.

"Merlot, I think but I haven't kept track."

"You're not a real redhead."

"Are you asking me or telling me?

"Didn't you take a turn at blonde."

"Sometimes I forget how long I've known you."

"Redheads have little patience with people who want to be redheads. Agree or disagree?"

"A redhead can go blonde, it's legal."

"But I suspect the life time of attention your red hair gets you makes it hard to give it up. Do redheads dye their hair."

"Ask a hairdresser."

"Your color serves you well."

"You're saying I didn't get as much attention when I was a blonde? You were always trying to feel me up."

"I wanted you on my resume. I still do."

"But I'm not a real redhead."

"I'll write your name in pencil."

"I can't think of anything worth saying." She strokes the back of my hand.

"I've lost count of how many times you've left me with this standing ovation."

"Whatever it is, add one more."

"Next week, please." I kiss her hand.

"As long as you enjoy my company, I'll enjoy yours."

"Promise not to change your hair."

Big Chief Larry

Sunrise Highway from Seaford to Massapequa is a line-up of unremarkable shops and storefronts. Then you confront Big Chief Larry. A 25-foot-tall cigar store Indian holding a peace pipe, he stands inside a square of cyclone fence no bigger than a dog run. Larry looks to the east - once home to his Shinnecock tribe.

One thing you don't find on Sunrise Highway is pedestrians. There are miles of sidewalk that hardly get walked on. Everyone on Long Island is driving to a place that has a parking lot. Standing on a corner of Sunrise you confuse passing motorists. Are they supposed to wait for you to cross or speed up to dissuade you from trying? People pull over as if you are wildlife spotted at a National Park.

Crossing at the light, I do a token trot suggesting I care about the drivers waiting for the light to change.

With two hundred dollars in my pocket, I'm not self-conscious. I'm solo in the Massapequa Diner. I take a booth in the back. The lunch crowd is coming in

"Coffee and rye toast, please." The waitress gives me a face that says "You're using up a lunch hour booth in my section for a coffee and toast? I have regulars."

A lost battalion of shattered men start to shuffle in and move as if to assigned tables. I don't see who I'm displacing until approached by too old bags carrying bags. I put my water down.

"Agnes isn't coming are you our third?" One asks.

"I'm happy to be Agnes." I invite them to sit.

The pair settle opposite me and after introductions, I ask them about the diner.

"They always give you too much." The twin on the right says.

"We used to come here with our husbands." The one on the left chips in.

Lunch appears – the kitchen knows they eat the same thing every week. I have coffee but no toast.

Old people will tell you things if you can make yourself listen. I approve of the career path of their grandchildren and congratulate them for putting up with each other.

"You don't know the half." They say it as one.

The one named Rose starts a story about hosting Thanksgiving dinner as a newlywed. She overhears her new brother-in-law on the phone.

"Mom can you believe she's using paper plates?"

"I had real utensils and glassware but who keeps a table setting for twelve? We weren't even married a year." She's pleading to me with tears in her eyes."

"From that day on I felt my marriage wouldn't survive. My mother-in law always had a look on her face that seemed to say 'Paper plates?"

Her partner Maureen scolds her.

"Rose, you've told that story a thousand times."

Spanish Philosophy

If philosophy doesn't improve daily living why pursue it? If the big picture doesn't help us focus on the picture at hand why bother? Insight into the floor plan should help on the dance floor. Philosophy must make the inevitable easier to accept.

I'm amused by the humiliation I feel watching her flirt with him in front of me. I can't blame her, he's leading man good looking. He's my buddy from the buddy system. We drank our first drinks together. He and I did a year in Guam then shore leave on a Med cruise. It's understood that he's better-looking than me but don't ask him to fix your car.

His wife and mine don't socialize so it's easy for us to cover for each other when we date girls at night school. We are both rowing oars under the G.I. Bill. Wives are off-limits, I thought, until we celebrate my wife's birthday at a City Island steakhouse.

"You're sitting very close for a guy who has been recently separated." I'm protesting his leaning toward my wife while he explains why his wife has flown to her mother's place in Arizona.

"We're in one of those fights where the first one to speak loses. I said I was sorry and told her I loved her but I said it in Spanish."

"After you get caught smooching a senorita?" My wife seems impressed by his recklessness.

"His wife doesn't understand him. You must have heard that before." I'm scolding my wife for flirting and the drinks are not an excuse.

"I don't want anything to put shade on your birthday. You're the woman I'm closest to at this moment." He touches his glass to hers and not mine.

"Yo, I'm sitting right here." I'm making a face of disbelief. My wife does nothing to disguise her cleavage. Both of them are giggling as he helps tie her bib.

Eating lobster is surgery and the two of them mock my pout as they exchange buttered forkfuls. When he stands to excuse himself, his lap is bulging.

"If I carried on like this with a woman you would throw a fit." I try to reason with her but her eyes are shining and her smile a mile wide.

"It's my birthday can he sleep over?"

"Why would I do that?"

"Pretend I'm one of your pets from night school."

"Are you accusing me of something?"

"Crime and punishment all in the same night." She laughs.

He returns from the men's room.

"Is everything settled?" He asks

"If you pay the check it is," she says.

"Gracias." He kisses her cheek

I assign myself no responsibility for the rest of the evening. What happens to him, what happens to her and what happens to me are separate issues.

There is no sense blaming anyone for anything. It's as if we are controlada por las estrellas.

I adopt a philosophy that I am not obliged to explain anything to anyone. Other than present circumstances I don't have circumstances. Keeping in mind that at any moment I could be squashed by a tour bus I don't dare a calendar. I strive to live each day as my first.

Dearest.

Where is the stationary I asked you for?

I don't deserve a letter but if you folded a blank sheet of paper and mailed it to me, it would have been be an amusing way of saying you have nothing to say.

You would need postage so a .37 cent stamp represents a sacrifice you don't want to make. I've enclosed a book of stamps that should last you a lifetime at the rate you're writing to me. I don't want to lie awake at night wondering if your handwriting has improved. Can you put a price on sound sleep?

Our boyfriend who was once my boyfriend dropped me a post card from Canada. He's working on a cruise ship where he's in charge of party balloons and dance music. Everything that's happened is in his rearview mirror. Why isn't it in ours?

Come back to me and I'll remind you of your infidelity every time we make love. We will replay the night you were an adult film star. You're a different girl when the lights are out. I can only offer you Hoy y manana.

Happy Birthday

Chalk and Cheese

She lay in bed listening to a rat tear through the baker's bag of biscotti she had left on the kitchen table. The snoring Soviet beside her couldn't drown out the passion of that rat repast. The asshole beside her had promised her windfalls from currency conversions and a catamaran cruise but he can't keep rodents out of his kitchen. She mourned her lost breakfast and ridiculous predicament. She was homesick for Latvia.

Her Mother had brought her to this crook's financial seminar. At first, he was hitting on her Mom then he was hitting on her. When her Mother flew home she stayed on at his village apartment. She had been living at the Waldorf so rats were the last thing on her mind.

The Caribbean catamaran cruise turned into a foursome - Anton's friend Miles and his girlfriend Sandy. As soon as they were a hundred yards off shore the boys urged the girls to go topless. When Miles strolled around with his flag at half- mast she demanded he put on a bathing suit. Drinking and sunburn turned their moods sour. Anton acted as Captain Bligh and wouldn't let them play music.

They docked at a party barge that had a bar and dance floor. She danced in her purple two piece determined to punish Anton for his boorish behavior. A black man stared holes into her as she seduced him onto the dance floor. Anton was livid when they got back to their boat. He fucked her on the aft netting slung inches above the applauding ocean.

At check-out Miles and Anton almost came to blows. Part of the charges wound up on her credit card. Anton's promise to repay her kept her at his side.

When the idea of ever seeing her money became a joke between them she broke his eyeglasses and caught a plane. She had overspent her allowance and had little to bring home to her divorced husband and boarding school son. On the way to Latvia she swore revenge on deadbeat Anton. Her Father was Latvian but her Mother was Sicilian. Don't steal money from a Sicilian.

There was a love letter waiting for her when she got home, another guy she had met at the seminar.

She remembered him staring at her. She had wrecked more than one meeting with her dramatic cleavage. It suggested a simple sneeze would unveil a nipple.

She wrote back suggesting they speak on the phone. After a month of international charges and time zone adjustments he invited her back to the states as his guest. She implied that his generosity would not go unrewarded.

"Never contact me again - you stupid cunt." This was Anton's last e-mail. She read it to her new host once they were settled in his bed.

"Anton fucked me out of $2500. I want you to help me get it back." In the aftermath of love-making it seemed like a plot to a movie.

When they returned to Anton's rat apartment the super said he had left with two months' rent outstanding. He suggested they try Staten Island because a selfie he had posted had a Statue of Liberty backdrop.

With her love letter writer, newly domesticated, they boarded the ferry in search of justice. The Russian community in Staten Island resides in a slice of St. George. With charm and plunging neckline she canvassed the local coffee shops and was directed to a home on Richmond Terrace where Anton's name appeared on a scrap of junk mail.

"What do you have mind?" Her freshly recruited sidekick saw a look on her face.

"You go ring his bell."

"And say what?"

"Be sure it's him. I showed you his picture. If he lets you in the house zap him with this." Smooth as a gunslinger she pulled a taser from her purse.

"Where did you get that?"

"On line."

"You're kidding me."

"You said you would help me. You said you loved me."

"I'm not a thug."

"Oh, so it's all bullshit. Saying you love me gets you laid. Don't make a fool out of me. Words are chalk this is cheese. It's time to pay for the pussy."

Climbing the steep staircase from the sidewalk to the front door he had a moment to consider the havoc writing a letter can create.

Garage Sale

A garage sale sign turns me onto a street I've never been on. A cul-de-sac shaped as an outer ear; every driveway stacked with the contents of attics, cellars and storage sheds. It's part garage sale part block party —neighbors perusing their neighbor's refuse.

I'm in search of the object that eludes me. I'm not sure what it is but I'm certain I will know it when I see it. A trinket, a bangle, something from a folding table that sets off a high, perhaps a figurine that shines a light. Anything used or carrying fingerprints is of interest. I'm a sucker for a book with notes in its margins.

I pick up a knickknack from Jamaica, the bathing beauty breasts border on poor taste. A corkscrew, a money clip, a chessboard blank as a historic battlefield, sit shoulder to shoulder on display. A toaster, a golf club a Diet Pepsi sign, I feel myself moving toward a decision by knowing what I don't want. I stub my toe on a barbell beneath a table. I pick up a small wooden elephant. There is no bad time to buy elephant.

I'm not proud of it but I used to wear a three- piece suit to work then change at my locker into the overalls issued to a baggage handler. My wife had told the neighbors I was airline executive. Guys at work would break my shoes about it. I tried to suggest I was selling insurance as a side job. They didn't believe that for a second. I couldn't produce a business card. I did it to spare my wife the embarrassment of having exaggerated.

When you move to Dix Hills don't think you're going to mow your lawn. Everybody has a landscaper and so will you. Keep your stoop neat and your garbage cans in a garbage can shed. You're in a burg of professional people – if you come outside it's to get into your car.

Jesus preached that we should love our neighbors. I don't even know my next-door neighbors but I love my wife. If she wants people to think I'm something I'm not I'll play along. It's nobody's business how a baggage handler bought a house in Dix Hills. You can ask all you want.

I add to cart, a nestling Mother and a book on motorcycle repair. It's a shopping success if I come home with an elephant, dolls within other dolls and a Zen discourse on stripped screws.

You're restricted in haggling if you're wearing a three-piece suit. I pay full price. At home I have a different relationship with my backyard neighbors than I do with my next-door neighbors. In my backyard I'm the real me – sitting in a chair, drinking beer and petting my wooden elephant. My wife hasn't told them anything about me. We haven't really been introduced. They mind their business and I mind mine.

Stores

I pipe aboard the USS Simon Lake as an E2 box-kicker sweeping storage compartments with a foxtail. As a nerdy newbie I'm assigned to a Master Chief. He advises me not to be caught standing still. His Catechism of storekeeping is reduced to two rules.

...If you can't find it you don't have it.

...Not what it is, where it is.

In a department as tightly organized as Stores a calming influence hangs in the air. Storekeepers tend to read, cooks like the movies, deck hands sleep at every opportunity. Aboard we move in our own worlds, ashore my mates are my blood brothers.

A black man in civilian clothes is eating a sandwich while sitting on the tailgate of his truck. I've come down to the pier to sign his paperwork. He's delivered a shipment of lightbulbs on a civilian bill of lading. We store 33 different types of lightbulbs on the Simon Lake - don't ask for one without knowing its part number.

On board there is no reward for the quick completion of assigned errands. When you're finished doing one thing you'll simply begin doing another. It's not like you can return to your rack and nap. You shouldn't complain in the company of anyone with a hash mark. Seamen are pawns, we move in one direction.

"Great day to be a civilian." I'm signing with a lifting autograph followed by printing my last name in capitals.

"Funny, I was envying you guys out sailing around on that mountain of steel."

"We look big in port Sir, out at sea we're a soap chip in an Olympic pool."

"I'm headed into two hours of stop and go traffic and another night with the old lady. I should have your problems, Swabbie."

"If you knew what they were you wouldn't say that."

Sea Story

All I ask is that you hold down that chair. Imagine an iceberg the size of a parking garage sitting dead center Sahara. A Stone Age ice castle dropped like a yolk on a breakfast griddle. It's a life-giving wet spot bobbing on a sea of sand. Under its influence a shoot of grass dares to shoot.

A white sail tacks on the blue horizon. I fire my last flare, its orange eye inviting rescue. Two of my crew are puking in the stern. A third lies dead and is weighing down our lifeboat. If we're still here in the morning I'll push him overboard. By then I'll have spent the longest night of my life.

My flare rises as a shot glass of light to the lips of the darkening sky. Stars switch on to support my toast. Light from outer space keeps the heavens bright as undersea darkness lifts off the ocean.

"You might as well wish for a geisha." Returning from the stern, Jack mocks my flare.

"No sense dying with a bullet in the chamber."

"Is that what we're doing?"

"I'd say we're pulling out all the stops Jacky. Before long we'll be tempted to eat this guy." I poke the deceased with my toe.

"What about the sailboat?"

"I'm sure they'll avoid us or assume it's fireworks."

"If they're stupid enough to pull alongside – we'll swap vessels."

"How do you know they won't rob us."

"Of what?"

"A pirate will always find something worth stealing. I know I always did."

"Till you found that underwater land mine."

"Don't blame me for the crap that's allowed to float around out here. Four hours out of port we shouldn't be running into a telephone pole."

The expiring flare cries its last orange tears. Certain as a steel overhead door, lights are out. Now every moment drags its feet.

I imagine us an ice boat bobbing on a sand dune. In a matter of hours, we will disappear. Jack and Newbie curl together in the throes of dehydration. I bail the best I can, scooping out seawater with my ballcap.

I loved my boat and now I love this lifeboat. I'm not ready to die but no one is looking for us. If we are found I don't think it will take a ton of police work to tie us to the mischief that has plagued the coast.

Shame

I'm overcome with guilt about not cleaning up after my dog. Earlier tonight, I was less sober than I am now. The dog deposit was lying on the curb steaming in moonlight. I let drinking cloud my judgement and skipped away. Even the dog frowned at me. I just couldn't scoop poop at that moment. I apologize, I'll do it in the morning but in the mean time I can't get to sleep under this cloud of remorse.

In the morning I drive by the scene of the crime. There it is - a slug belted by gamma rays. It remains intact and as obvious as a nose pimple. I can't expect anyone else to help - this isn't a fucking Snickers lying there. I'll need a doubled plastic bag and a place to ditch the body. With my business suit on I don't feel like walking down the block with a turd in my hand. I'll get it on the way home from work. In the mean time I have to ask my wife what she's feeding the dog. That animal has defiled the neighborhood.

I'm getting neighborhood side eyes on my way home. Work was so crazy I forgot I had a date with dog doo. I could walk Free back there and kill two turds with one scoop but I'll do it after dark. I'm not the only dog owner - nobody can hang me unless they have surveillance.

As I walk our usual route, Free pulls me toward last night's late deposit. Neighbors are coming outside and shining flashlights at me. Is this a thing? Is that how you censor people who don't clean up after their dog in Dix Hills? I'm a man who slings luggage in the belly of an aircraft while wearing earmuffs and knee pads. What's it to you if I let a shit sit overnight?

At the park the body is missing. I clean up after Free while wondering what Good Samaritan has covered for me. Back home I find the answer on my stoop. Wrapped in swaddling paper towel the abandoned passage has returned to its author. Free barks to claim ownership.

Also by Pete Kearney

RING SONGS

HITCHIN TO SEA LEVEL

STORY AVENUE

MCMURDO

ALL BRAND NEW